A Gift of Love to:

_____

on this date of:

_____

From:

_____

'Twas the Night of Christ's Birth

by
Donna Miles

Photography by
Walden's House of Photography

Booksmiles Press — Lexington, Kentucky

Booksmiles Press
P. O. Box 24140
Lexington, KY 40524 - 4140

ISBN 0 - 9671903 - 0 - 4

00 01 02 03 04   5 4 3 2 1

Printed on acid-free paper for greater permanence and durability.
Hardbound limited edition

Production by Four Colour Imports, Ltd.
Louisville, Kentucky
Printed in China

Dedication

To my mom, Anna, who as a young widow raised me
and my seven siblings with great courage, strength, and
Christian faith, and who enticed us as children to read
and recite poetry during our summer break
with the incentive of earning a quarter!

And to my husband and best friend, David, who
along with our kids, Adam and Jessica, encouraged
me in the long process of bringing my story to print.

'Twas the Night of Christ's Birth

'Twas the night of Christ's birth,
And all through Bethlehem,
Not a creature was stirring,
Not even a lamb.

The prayers were all said
By the families with care
In hopes that salvation
Soon would be theirs.

The children were nestled
All snug in their beds
While visions of Baby Jesus
Danced in their heads.

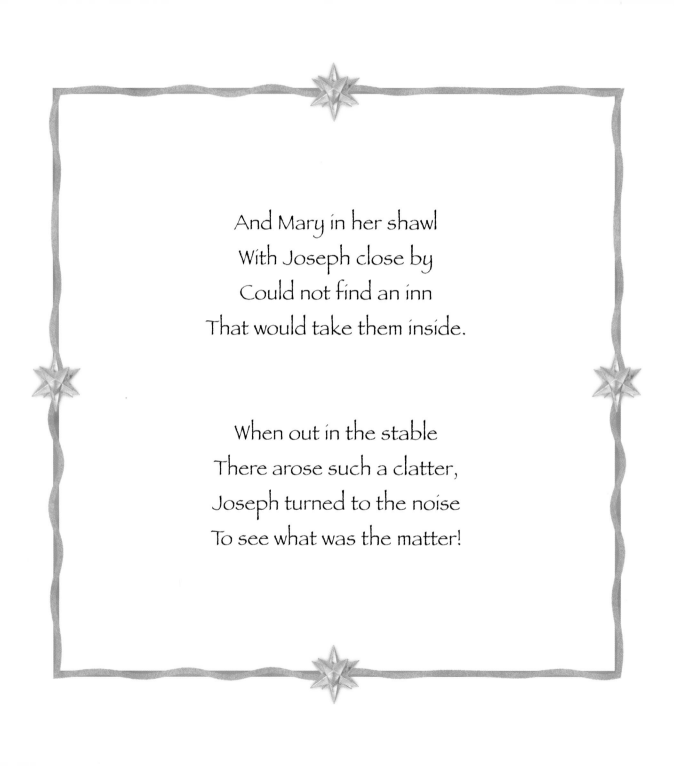

And Mary in her shawl
With Joseph close by
Could not find an inn
That would take them inside.

When out in the stable
There arose such a clatter,
Joseph turned to the noise
To see what was the matter!

Away to the stable
He hurried along
Leading the donkey
That Mary sat on.

The star shone so brightly,
The town was aglow,
For a miracle from God
Was about to unfold.

It was there in the stable
With cows, goats, and sheep,
The birth of Lord Jesus —
A promise He'd keep

To deliver us all
From our sins if we'd try
To love one another
Till the day that we die.

More rapid than moonbeams
The angels they came,
And they sang with great joy
As they called out His name.

O Jesus, our Savior,
O Emmanuel!
Today is your birthday.
Let's all give a yell!

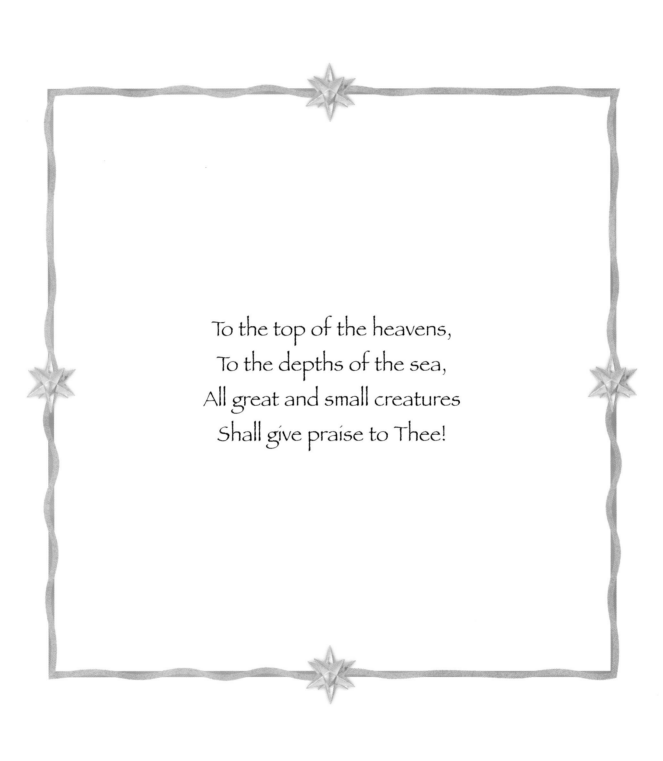

To the top of the heavens,
To the depths of the sea,
All great and small creatures
Shall give praise to Thee!

As dry leaves that before
A wild hurricane fly,
When they meet with an obstacle
Mount to the sky,

So the news of the birth
Was spread far and wide,
And God's people were at peace
As they stood side by side.

The angels laughed softly
As the little Babe cried,
While Mary and Joseph
Just looked on with pride,

For they knew He was special,
They had no need to fear.
This blessed event brought
Our heavenly God near.

He was wrapped all in cloth
From His feet to His head,
And was happy to rest
In His wee manger bed.

His home was not fancy,
In fact, it was plain -
The same place the cows,
Sheep, and donkeys had lain.

His eyes, how they twinkled
As He lay so content,
Fulfilling the promise
That God's Son would be sent.

His tiny red mouth
Was drawn up like a bow,
And His innocent pureness
Made His face all aglow.

The angels went out
To proclaim the good news.
The shepherds, they found,
Were taking a snooze!

The shepherds and sheep
Came down from the hill
To pray at the barn door,
So quiet and still.

The star grew so brilliant
The wisemen, they say,
Traveled long days and nights,
from far, far away.

Alongside their camels
And with rare gifts in hand,
They crossed over mountains
And vast desert lands.

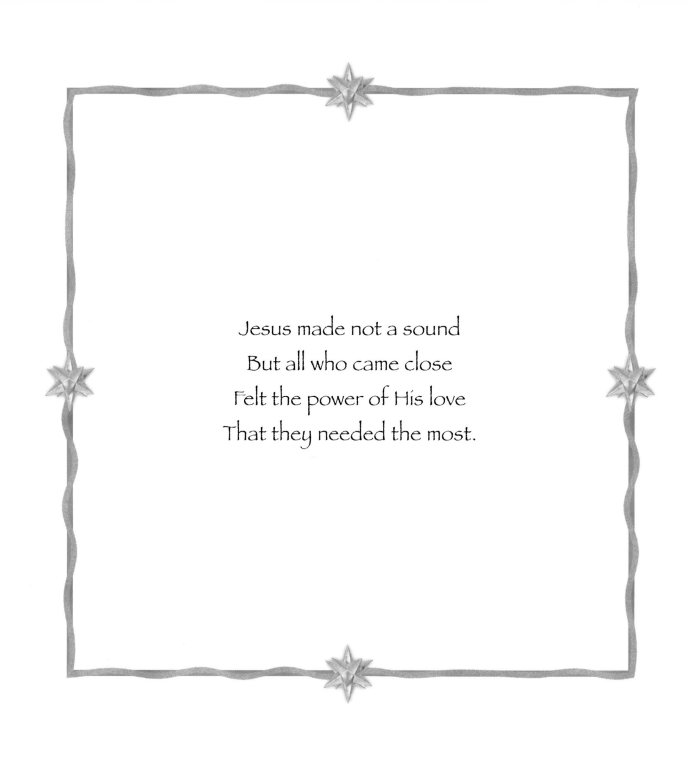

Jesus made not a sound
But all who came close
Felt the power of His love
That they needed the most.

And so - to this day
We sing songs and give presents,
That we may, in some way
Feel His holy presence.

May we always remember
His example of love,
For He gave of Himself
And still gives from above.

So go forth today
With joy in your heart,
And from
FAITH, HOPE, And LOVE
may you never depart!

SPECIAL THANKS

To my dear friends at Walden's House of Photography for the creation of such wonderful photographic images. Tim and Beverly, your photographic talents along with your enthusiasm and creative guidance for this project have been a true blessing. To each one of the staff members with whom I have worked over the years, I send a big hug and lots of love!

To Sean Sears and Rae Ella House for their artistic talents in the field of graphic design and with whose help the project developed into true book form.

To teachers Kari Boneau, Linda Thompson, and Sally Wilkinson for their proofing and suggestions throughout the book and to Georgiana Strickland for the final copy editing.

To all of my big family and friends who were both critics and cheerleaders along the way. You are the best!

To Father Greg Schuler of Christ the King Cathedral for his kind words of encouragement, and to Sr. Clara Fehringer for her help in one of the photo shoots.

With an extra special thanks to all of God's children who participated in the photos, and their families who gave of their time so generously.

Acknowledgments

An acknowledgment is due to the author, Clement C. Moore, whose spirit lives on in his wonderful story and whose poetry I have made so much use of in this book.

To see more award-winning portraits and for information on upcoming classes and seminars by Walden's House of Photography, visit them on the web at www.waldensphotography.com

The Kentucky-crafted, soft sculptured creatures shown in this book were created by the Country Nouveau Company. For more information about these and other whimsical characters contact Angela B. Shocklee at 270-486-3272 or write to:
Country Nouveau Company, 360 Morris Road, Island, KY 42350

Additional copies of this book may be
ordered by contacting:

Booksmiles Press, Dept. DC
P.O. Box 24140
Lexington, KY 40524 - 4140
(859) 273-4135

Or visit us at our web site at
www.booksmiles.com